SEVEN DEADLY SINS, SEVEN LIVELY VIRTUES

STUDY GUIDE

A Catholic Study Program presented by
BISHOP ROBERT BARRON

Study Guide written by
MARK P. SHEA

SECOND EDITION

WORD on FIRE

www.WORDONFIRE.org
© 2015 Word on Fire Catholic Ministries

✠

SEVEN DEADLY SINS, SEVEN LIVELY VIRTUES

TABLE OF CONTENTS

OPPORTUNITIES
FOR ADDITIONAL STUDY

The best accompaniment to this study guide is to read Dante Alighieri's great poem *The Divine Comedy*. Born in 1265 and raised in a prominent family in Florence, Italy, Dante became the greatest poet of the Middle Ages, albeit through much suffering after his permanent exile from his home city in 1301, resulting from a political dispute. His exile lasted until his death in 1321.

Extremely learned, not only in poetry but in philosophy, theology, politics and the science of the day, Dante created in *The Divine Comedy* a poem that is, at once, a great story of an epic journey through Hell, up Mount Purgatory, and into Heaven—as well as an exploration of the great truths concerning human nature, our relationship with God, and the soul's journey to happiness. Dante is a master architect and constructs his poem in such a way that each image not only "works" to support the story, but also represents multiple layers of allegorical truth about the human condition and the ways of God.

There are numerous translations available with copious explanatory notes. We would recommend the translation by Robert and Jean Hollander from Doubleday. It is available in most bookstores or online from outlets such as Amazon.com. In addition, you can access the Hollanders' translation online at http://etcweb.princeton.edu/dante/pdp/.

INTRODUCTION

Welcome to Bishop Robert Barron's enlightening study on sin and virtue. Over the course of this study, we will be taking a look at what Catholic tradition calls the Seven Deadly Sins and contrasting them with what Bishop Barron refers to as the Seven Lively Virtues.

This guide is designed to help you apply to your life what you will learn from Bishop Barron's look at the Catholic tradition. The aim is to increase understanding, promote reflection, and encourage practical action. You will have the chance to dig into the Catholic tradition and grapple with Scripture and the Church's teaching as it is summarized in *The Catechism of the Catholic Church.* You will also be able to use the materials provided in Bishop Barron's DVD in order to assess and enhance your life as a disciple of Jesus Christ. The guide is built around QUESTIONS FOR UNDERSTANDING and QUESTIONS FOR REFLECTION, which will reinfoce the main points made in each section on a Deadly Sin and its corresponding Lively Virtue.

Throughout the study, you will be asked to reference different Bible verses and passages. We recommend the *New American Bible* or the *Revised Standard Version*, or you can also use another acceptable Catholic translation. To answer the questions, you will need to refer to the *Catechism of the Catholic Church*, which can be purchased at your local bookstore or found online at: www.scborromeo.org/ccc.htm.

So without further ado, let's take a look at Bishop Barron's introductory remarks and then consider the questions on the following pages.

QUESTIONS FOR UNDERSTANDING

1. Read the *Catechism of the Catholic Church* (CCC) paragraphs 1849-1851 and 1866. What is sin? What are the Seven Deadly Sins?

2. Read CCC 1803 and Philippians 4:8. What is virtue? Why is it important in the spiritual life?

3. Read Wisdom 1. What are the qualities of wisdom? What are the qualities of the wise or righteous person? What are the qualities of the unwise fool?

4. Read CCC 759. As a sheer, gratuitous gift, God intends that you exist and share in his divine life. What response does this require from us?

QUESTIONS FOR REFLECTION

1. The startling proposition, "God does not need you" affects different people in different ways. Some people might feel relief. Others might feel resentment. Still others might feel puzzlement. What is your response to that proposition?

2. St. Thomas Aquinas says that love is "willing the good of the other as other." Can you think of examples of this that you have witnessed either in your own life or in the lives of others? Can you describe an experience of having been a conduit for God's love?

3. Bishop Barron also warns of the opposite danger of a "love" that is really "indirect egotism." Can you think of times in your life when you have "loved" somebody in order to get him/her to do something for you and not because you actually cared about his/her good? Or, how about a time when your relationship with a person took precedence over your relationship with God? How did you recognize and overcome temptations like this?

4. Bishop Barron describes fear as being at the root of all sin. Have you ever experienced fear working against the virtue of love in your life? How can fear lead you to forget the love of God and put your trust somewhere else?

5. What makes sin deadly? How can God's anger be good news for us? Have you ever experience sin's killing effect? Have you ever seen God's liberation from that deadliness at work in your life? What was that like?

PRIDE & HUMILITY

The souls on Mount Purgatory in Dante's *Divine Comedy* do various forms of penance for their sins in ways that reflect both the nature of their sins and the way to salvation from those sins. The proud bear heavy rocks on their backs which simultaneously weigh them down (as pride weighs us down) and force them to look at the earth from which they came. This reveals the quintessential truth about our lives: we are "of the earth" and not the creators of good and evil, right and wrong. To learn humility is to learn to live in reality. In this study guide, be particularly attentive to how you can learn to live in reality, forsake pride, and humble yourself.

QUESTIONS FOR UNDERSTANDING

1. Read Matthew 5:3, 2 Corinthians 8:9, Proverbs 16:18-19 and CCC 2546. What does it mean to be "poor in spirit"? How does this attitude contrast with pride? How does Jesus model this? How can we imitate that in practical ways?

2. Read CCC 2547. Can the proud truly abandon themselves to "the providence of the Father"? Why or why not?

3. Read CCC 2631. How can pride stand in the way of forgiveness, prayer, and right worship?

4. Read Philippians 2:1-11. What qualities does Paul encourage us to have? How does he base this command on Jesus Christ? What did Jesus do, according to Paul?

5. Read Luke 1:46-55. How does Mary model humility? What are some of the things Mary says that our culture does not tend to identify as "humble" statements? How does this illuminate the differences between the biblical understanding of humility and our cultural notions of it?

QUESTIONS FOR REFLECTION

1. Bishop Barron mentions the famous "mystery clause" from the Supreme Court's "Casey Decision," which declares: "At the heart of liberty is the right to define one's own concept of existence, of meaning, of the universe, and of the mystery of human life." How does this understanding of freedom differ from a Christian understanding? What are some of the consequences of this understanding of freedom?

2. Dante puts pride at the bottom of Mount Purgatory as the heaviest and deadliest sin to be purged. Have you ever thought of pride as the worst sin, or do you tend to think other sins are worse? Why is pride the worst sin? How have you seen pride at work in your life?

3. Dante represents the penance for pride as carrying heavy boulders on the back. Have you had to suffer for pride? What was it like? Has God brought healing out of that suffering? What was that like?

4. Humility is described variously as being "earthy," or living in truth, or being self-forgetful. How and when have you experienced these things? Have you ever known a humble person? What was he or she like?

5. A good first step toward cultivating the virtue of humility is to purposely take the lower place and not merely the equal place to somebody else. Aristotle uses the image of bending the stick backward, not merely bending it straight. Have you ever put yourself lower than a competitor? Is there somebody in your life to whom you need to cede the higher place? What concrete step could you take to do that?

ENVY & ADMIRATION

As we continue climbing Mount Purgatory, we come to the second level, where Envy, the daughter of Pride, is purged. Envy is pleasure in the sorrow of another and resentment over their happiness or success. It is, like all the deadly sins, a "capital" or "head" sin because it is a fountain from which other evil acts flow; acts such as theft, betrayal, and even murder. Both Scripture and the great literature of the world often speak to us of the deadly effects of envy. They remind us that our true happiness is found by joining our lives in love with God and others, who also have been loved into being by God.

QUESTIONS FOR UNDERSTANDING

1. Read Isaiah 26:12 and Philippians 2:12-13. Who should receive the glory for every good thing we do? How does Paul understand the way in which we should view our accomplishments in light of our relationship to God?

2. Read 1 Corinthians 12:4-31. How does Paul say that we are to understand our relationship to one another and the relative importance of our contributions?

3. Read Galatians 5:14-26. What is the source of what Paul sees: envy, competition, pride, self-conceit, vying for position and status, factionalism, drunkenness, and other such sins? What is the result of giving in to these sins? What does Paul tell us is the only way to defeat these sins? How do we put that into practice?

4. Read CCC 2538-2540. How does the tenth commandment illuminate the sin of envy in the heart? What does St. John Chrysostom prescribe as the best medicine for killing the sin of envy?

QUESTIONS FOR REFLECTION

1. Have you ever felt resentment over somebody's success or joy over his or her failure? If so, do you still struggle with it, or did you defeat that in your heart? How?

2. Why is envy the daughter of pride and not, say, avarice or gluttony?

3. Dante's penance for the envious is that they have their eyes sewn shut as medieval falconers would sew shut the eyes of their falcons. How is this both a punishment and a medicine for the envious? What does this tell us about the sin of envy?

4. Have you ever had a hero or someone you deeply admired? Who was it and why did you admire him or her so much? If you could meet him or her, what would you say? Can you contrast the admiration you have had for a hero with an experience of envy you have had for a competitor?

5. Can you think of one person in your life who you need to "go out of your way" to praise? Have you ever, like John the Baptist, said of another you were tempted to envy, "He must increase, and I must decrease?" Have you ever had a sense of contentment in knowing where you begin and where you end without having to compare yourself to others?

NOTES:

ANGER & FORGIVENESS

Because hurt is everywhere, anger is everywhere. Scripture tells us "Be angry but do not sin" (Ephesians 4:26). This surprising advice from St. Paul points to the truth about anger: namely, that it is a normal part of human existence (like hunger) and that it is not sinful except when taken to excess. St. Thomas describes the sin of anger as an unreasonable, irrational, and immoderate desire for vengeance. Given our fallen condition, this is quite common. When somebody hurts us, we don't want mere justice that responds in equal measure to the sin we have suffered. We want overwhelming retaliation that destroys our enemy. This is why, for instance, the law of Moses finds it necessary to prescribe "eye for eye, tooth for tooth, hand for hand, foot for foot, burn for burn, wound for wound, stripe for stripe" (Exodus 21:24-25). It's not because ancient Israelites were barbarians radically different from us. It's because they were barbarians just like us who would, if they could, render an arm and a leg for a foot, a life for an eye, or a life for a wound. The law of Moses was given in order to rein in our thirst to up the ante in the cycle of violence. But it was more than the law of Moses could do to break that cycle. Only Jesus can wash away the sin of the world by letting sin spend itself on him and then swallowing it up in mercy.

We must do likewise.

QUESTIONS FOR UNDERSTANDING

1. Read Mark 3:1-5, John 2:13-17 and CCC 1765. Is anger always a sin? When is anger justified and when is it a sin?

2. Read Matthew 26:50-54 and Luke 22:50-51. How does Jesus confront evil? How does Peter confront evil? What are the differences? According to Bishop Barron, what do the Fathers of the Church see imaged in this incident that teaches us about the difference between the sin of anger and the grace of God?

3. Read Romans 12:17-21. How does this way of confronting evil demonstrate both the power and humility of God? To whom does vengeance belong, and as such, how are we to respond when it seems that vengeance is needed?

4. Read Matthew 6:9-15 and Matthew 18:23-34. What is the condition Jesus puts on the prayer for forgiveness in the Our Father? What is the promise and the warning of that condition? What does the parable of the Unmerciful Servant suggest about the importance of the slights we receive compared with our sins that God has forgiven?

5. Read Colossians 3:12-13. What is the root and basis of our forgiveness of one another? How does St. Paul say we should treat one another because of this root of forgiveness?

QUESTIONS FOR REFLECTION

1. Dante pictures the penitent angry as being inundated with smoke. How is anger like smoke? How can anger cloud our vision? How have you "cleared the air" of anger with somebody through forgiveness?

2. Bishop Barron says that forgiveness involves more than mere thought or a change in attitude, such as "not wishing harm on somebody." Forgiveness requires breaking the cycle of violence by letting evil spend itself and be met with love and mercy. He gives examples of the non-violent resistance of Martin Luther King, Jr. and of Gandhi. Have you ever been in a situation where you or somebody you know turned the other cheek? What was that like? What was the result?

3. Can you think of places in our culture where the forgiveness of sins is rejected as "weak" or wrong? How can we make it clear that forgiveness and mercy are the ultimate examples of the power of God?

4. Is there somebody in your life that you need to forgive? What one positive, concrete step can you take today to confront your sin of anger with the forgiving power of Christ?

NOTES:

SLOTH & ZEAL

When we come to the Cornice of the Slothful, we come to the "dead center" of the entire Divine Comedy, midway up Mount Purgatory and midway through the poem. This place, like the eye of a hurricane, is the fitting spot to discuss sloth, which St. Thomas defined as sorrow or indifference to spiritual good, and which medieval people called the "noonday devil." Sloth is when a human heart becomes bored with and inert to the things of God. It is not the same thing as mere laziness. A person can be mired in the depths of sloth while filled with energy for video games, TV, workaholism, money, and all the other distractions the world provides to keep us numb to the voice of God and the desire for happiness and holiness. Bishop Barron reminds us that the antidote for sloth is zeal for God. This is best kindled by fervent prayer for God to reveal our mission in life, coupled with the vigorous pursuit of the corporal and spiritual works of mercy.

QUESTIONS FOR UNDERSTANDING

1. Read Psalm 73. In what ways is the psalmist tempted to be slothful? How does he deal with these temptations, and what does he conclude?

2. Read CCC 2733. What is "presumption," and how does acedia (that is, sloth) work to attack and break down our prayer life? How is this destructive of a relationship with the living God?

3. Read Luke 1:39-45. As they run in Dante's Purgatory, Luke 1:39 is the passage the penitent slothful hear. Why was Mary in haste? Who was she going to see? What does this image show us about Christian calling?

4. Read CCC 2447. What are the corporal (bodily) and spiritual works of mercy? Why are they important to our spiritual life?

5. Read Matthew 25:31-46. Does Jesus see the corporal works of mercy as something strictly for "religious" people? Does Jesus see our works of mercy mattering only if we do them for "religious" people?

QUESTIONS FOR REFLECTION

1. Have you or someone you know ever been indifferent to the workings of God? What are the characteristics of that indifference? How can it be overcome?

2. People often confuse the sin of sloth with laziness. Bishop Barron points out that frenetic interest in the things of this world can often mask our indifference to the things of the Spirit. Have you ever found yourself wrapped up in extreme busyness? What was that like? What did you do to fight it and make sure it didn't separate you from the things of the Spirit?

3. One aspect of sloth is the tendency to say that truth doesn't matter. Are there places in your life or in the surrounding culture where relativism and the denial of truth are used as a kind of escape hatch for responsibility? How can this be fought?

4. Review the list of corporal and spiritual works of mercy from Q. 4 above. Where do you practice the corporal and spiritual works of mercy in your life? Are there particular works of mercy that you focus on? Why? Are there particular works of mercy you neglect? Why?

5. In John 2:13-21, Jesus' zeal for the house of God led him to drive out the moneychangers from the temple and make clear that the true temple was not a stone building, but the temple of his body. In what ways can you be filled with zeal for the house of God, which is the Church?

AVARICE & GENEROSITY

Dante's continuing journey up Mount Purgatory means he is becoming lighter, freer and less burdened by sin. In arriving at the Cornice of the Penitent Avaricious, we are looking at a sin which, while less serious than pride, envy, anger and sloth, is still deadly, as are all the capital sins. It is, after all, avarice that sends the rich man to hell in Jesus' parable of Lazarus and the Rich Man. St. Thomas tells us that avarice is the immoderate or unreasonable desire for riches. It is not wrong to own property or to make a profit. Sin only enters into the situation when we love these created things more than we love God or our neighbor. The moment we care more about riches than about how to use those riches for the common good is the moment we are opening the door to avarice. Conversely, the moment we start recognizing our wealth as a gift of God given to us both for our good and for the good of our neighbor—and begin finding ways to share that wealth with our neighbor—is the day we begin to live generously and imitate God, who became poor for our sake that we might become rich.

QUESTIONS FOR UNDERSTANDING

1. Read Matthew 6:19-34 and 1 Timothy 6:6-10. What is the attitude we are to take toward the wealth of this world? What can happen if we relentlessly pursue wealth, "longing to be rich"? What are "treasures in heaven"?

2. Read Luke 16:19-31. How much importance does Jesus place on generosity to the poor?

3. Read CCC 1906-1909. What is meant by the "common good"? What is our personal responsibility for contributing to the common good?

4. Read 2 Corinthians 8:1-15. How does Paul urge the Corinthians to be generous? How does he preserve their freedom and yet call them to give? In verse 15, he cites the story of the manna in the wilderness in Exodus 16. How does this picture of the common good relate to our own use of riches today?

QUESTIONS FOR REFLECTION

1. Avarice is often thought of as a sin of the rich and, to be sure, many rich people are afflicted with this temptation. However, a poor person can also be obsessed with money (and with envy of the rich). Have you ever struggled with an inordinate desire for riches? How does our culture encourage the love of money? How can you overcome this temptation?

2. Pope Leo XIII taught us that once the demands of necessity and propriety have been met, the rest of our wealth belongs to the poor. What is your honest reaction to that? Reflect on the "demands of necessity and propriety" in your own circumstances and whether you should be giving more away.

3. Have you ever been poor yourself and found it necessary to rely on the help of others to get by? What was that like? Did you feel gratitude? Shame? Determination to change your circumstances? Were you able to share with others in some way even when you had little?

4. Jesus says of the poor widow who put two tiny copper coins in the temple treasury that she gave more than all those who had contributed out of their excess. Have you or somebody you know ever given sacrificially? Describe the situation and comment on the outcome of that gift, both to the receiver and to the giver.

5. Dante's penitents are purged of the sin of avarice by being fettered face down on the earth. Because avarice looks no further than the accumulation of wealth or its lavish spending on worldly pleasure, the punishment fits the sin: penitents must look only at the earth upon which they wasted their wealth. Have you ever had a time when you realized that you could never get enough of what you thought you wanted? If so, how did this realization affect your priorities?

NOTES:

GLUTTONY & ASCETICISM

As we continue climbing Mount Purgatory, we become freer of the heavy sins and begin to encounter the lighter ones. This does not make them less deadly, of course, but it does mean that these sins involve "less grave" perversions of the good. Pride, envy and anger are perverted loves that delight in harm to others. Sloth is *defective* love that fails to take an interest in the things of God. Gluttony, however, is an excess of love for created things, particularly food and drink, over the love of God. It is lighter because the glutton at least loves something. But it remains deadly because the love is not in right relationship to the love of God or the love of neighbor. We live in a culture of gluttony. Our culture makes it extremely easy to believe that "we deserve a break today," and we should continually indulge our appetites (the appetite for food being only one of the many). Our faith does not call us to reject food and drink as bad things, but only to use them within reason and with respect for the common good and the love of God and others. As we look at the sin of gluttony and its antidote, asceticism, pay attention to ways in which you may be tempted toward excessive love of food and drink. Also, consider models you may have seen of people with a balanced and moderate approach to their appetites. Ask God for the grace to acquire self-discipline so that you can have the happiness you truly desire.

QUESTIONS FOR UNDERSTANDING

1. Read Genesis 3 and Matthew 4:1-4. What is the devil trying to get Jesus to do? How does this parallel Satan's temptation of Adam and Eve? How does Jesus answer the Tempter? How can you apply the passage Jesus cites from Deuteronomy 8:3 to your life?

2. Read Matthew 11:16-19. What do Jesus' enemies accuse him of? What does this suggest about Jesus' attitude toward the goodness of food and drink? What does it suggest about the attitudes of his enemies?

3. Read Matthew 6:16-21. What is to be our attitude as we fast? How does this relate to Bishop Barron's point that gluttony is the attempt to gain happiness from sources that can't give it to us? How do fasting and prayer directly challenge this disordered desire?

4. Read Isaiah 58. How does God tell Israel to make a fast pleasing to him? What does God promise us when we fast in the spirit he desires?

QUESTIONS FOR REFLECTION

1. Do you or somebody you know struggle with enslavement to excessive love of food and/or drink? Do you know people with the opposite problem: a fear of eating? How do these disordered appetites push the love of God and neighbor out of the center of our lives?

2. There's an expression: "You can never get enough of what you don't really want." Have you ever experienced using food as a way of trying to fill an inner emptiness that God is meant to fill? Did you overcome it? How?

3. Bishop Barron compares asceticism to using a Stairmaster so that you can become healthier. In the spiritual life, we are likewise called to asceticism to discipline our appetites and become spiritually healthier by opening our lives to God. Have you ever tried an ascetic practice such as fasting? What were the benefits you gained?

4. Have you ever tried making a deliberate sacrifice of something you love, not out of an attempt to "diet" but as an offering to God and for his Church? What did you do and what happened when you did?

NOTES:

LUST & CHASTITY

C.S. Lewis once remarked that he was a converted pagan living in a country of apostate Puritans. He was speaking of Britain, but much the same could be said of American culture as well. Our apostate Puritan culture has long taught us to believe that the very worst sin in the world is lust. But Dante regards lust as the lightest and least serious of the deadly sins. It is, like gluttony, an excess of love for *something* rather than the choice to reject love. What it is not, however, is an excess of love for another person, despite the fact that it involves sex. That's the main problem with it: lust is the sin of treating another person as a means to an end. Lewis remarks that the lustful man does not "want a woman." He wants an experience for which the woman happens to be the necessary apparatus. In short, lust treats people like things and insults the love they are due as human beings. In this study, pay attention to the ways in which you have been tempted (or given in to the temptation) to treat human beings as things and not persons. Pay attention, as well, to the ways in which God is calling you out of the prison of lust so that you may truly be filled with God's love and respect for your neighbor.

QUESTIONS FOR UNDERSTANDING

1. Read Matthew 5:27-30. Where does Jesus see lust beginning? Jesus uses hyperbole to point out the need for radical repentance from the sin of lust. Why is such drastic action demanded? What does this suggest about the addictive nature of lust?

2. John Paul II warned that people can commit the sin of lust even *within* marriage. What do you think he meant?

3. Read 1 Corinthians 6:12-20. God has made you so that his love can surge through you and enable you to love others for their own sake and not for your use and exploitation. Given that, why does Paul find lust so grave a sin against Christ?

4. Read I John 2:15-17. What does John mean by "lust"? How does it relate to pride? What does John say about this world and its relationship to lust?

5. Read CCC 2392-2400. What is chastity? Who is the model of chastity? What is the difference between chastity and celibacy?

QUESTIONS FOR REFLECTION

1. What are some of the temptations in our culture toward lust? What are some ways we can arm ourselves against these temptations?

2. Have you ever had an experience of falling in love? How was it different from mere lust?

3. People talk about pornography as a "victimless crime." Do you agree with this statement? Why or why not?

4. Dante's penitent lustful must pass through fire to be cleansed of this sin. How is this again a punishment that fits the sin? What in your life needs to be burned up in order to free you from the sin of lust?

5. Do you know some model—whether in Scripture, among the saints, or in your life—of the practice of joyful chastity? What concrete step could you take today to imitate that?

BIOGRAPHICAL INFORMATION

BISHOP ROBERT BARRON

Bishop Robert Barron is an acclaimed author, speaker, and theologian. He is the founder of Word on Fire Catholic Ministries and from 2012 until 2015 served as the Rector-President of Mundelein Seminary/University of St. Mary of the Lake. Ordained in 1986 in the Archdiocese of Chicago, he now serves as an auxiliary bishop in the Archdiocese of Los Angeles.

Bishop Barron received a Master's Degree in Philosophy from The Catholic University of America in 1982 and a Doctorate in Sacred Theology from the Institut Catholique de Paris in 1992.

Bishop Barron's apostolate, Word on Fire Catholic Ministries, exists to draw people into the Body of Christ, which is the Church, and thereby give them access to all the gifts that Jesus wants his people to enjoy. To be most effective in this mission, Word on Fire places an emphasis and urgency on the use of contemporary forms of media and innovative communication technologies.

MARK P. SHEA

Mark P. Shea is a popular Catholic writer and speaker. Mark was raised as an agnostic, became a non-denominational Evangelical in 1979, and entered the Catholic Church in 1987.

Mark's most recent work is *Mary, Mother of the Son* (Marytown). He contributes articles to many periodicals, including his popular column "Connecting the Dots" for the *National Catholic Register* and his daily blog on Patheos.com. He is also a frequent blogger at *Catholic and Enjoying It!* and at the *Register*. Mark is known nationally for his one minute "Words of Encouragement" on Catholic radio and he has also appeared numerous times on television. In addition, Mark is an internationally known speaker on various issues in Catholic faith and life.

Mark lives in Washington State with his wife, Janet, and their four sons.